Barcelona
The city of Gaudí

Text
Llàtzer Moix

Photography
Pere Vivas · Ricard Pla · Jordi Todó

Lluís Bertran · Lluís Casals · Albert Heras · Jordi Llobet · Jordi Longas
Manel Pérez · Ramon Pla · Juanjo Puente · Jordi Puig · Miguel Raurich
Siqui Sánchez · Jaume Serrat · Pere Sintes · Tino Soriano

Illustrations
Perico Pastor

TRIANGLE ▼ POSTALS

Barcelona, the greatest of the Mediterranean capitals, prepares itself for the third millennia of its history with enthusiasm, energy and a renovated image. The 1992 Olympic Games gave rise, during the nineteen eighties, to a spectacular process of widespread development. The city has preserved its traditional attractions, its open and hospitable character, temperate climate with an average temperature of 17ºC, its architectural treasures and natural surroundings, but, at the same time, has undergone a complete modernisation which includes the building of the new airport, new residential areas with leisure and service facilities, the renovation of its communication services and, also, the rejuvenation of its urban façade.

A visitor returning to Barcelona after a ten year absence will find a very different and vastly improved metropolis. This book reflects on both the city's history and its extraordinary present and, through a superb collection of images, offers the reader an accurate portrait of the new Barcelona.

The city through the ages

Barcino was founded as a Roman colony more than two thousand years ago. They chose to build the city in a sandy enclave on the northeastern Iberian coast, situated between the mouths of two rivers – the Llobregat and the Besós – and protected by the Collserola mountain range. The strategic position of the first settlement, well communicated both by water and by land, with a sea port and walls, was well suited for a capital city. The benign climate and abundance of of natural

1. Roman mosaic, the Three Graces (300-400 A.D.) Museu d'Arqueologia de Catalunya.

1

1

2

3

resources were to do the rest, and, over the centuries, the city became the capital of Catalunya and Spain's principal trading port.

The history of Barcelona is closely linked to that of the Catalan nation and, in turn to that of the Catalan language which is fruit of the evolution of Latin (more related to Provençal French than Castilian Spanish), and a cohesive element in the traditions, culture and identity of the country. One of the city's greatest moments took place in the Middle Ages when the different fiefs united as the County of Barcelona under the French kings, and this unification gave rise to the great Catalan expansion throughout the Mediterranean in the 13th and 14th centuries. Traces of these commercial and military feats can still be seen today in many places, for example Sicily, Malta, Sardinia and even

1 & 2. Mural painting of a dome from Barcino (4th century). Stoneware male figure from stone of Montjuïc (I B.C. - I A.D.) Museu d'Història de la Ciutat.
3. Roman remains. Centre Excursionista.
4. Map of old Barcelona, 1576 A.D.

BARCELONA

BARCINO, quæ vulgo Barcelona dicitur, vrbs est apud Hispanos celeberrima, mediterranei maris
litori, situ nobilitata, mirâq; antiquitatem redolet. A Romanis in Hispaniam transmissis, Fauentia
dicta Multis abinc sæculis, cum diuersæ exterarum nationum manus, sese per Hispanias effunderent,
hanc etiam vrbem, inter alias solo æquarunt, quæ proin vasta perseuerauit, donec eam noui
incolæ iterum instaurarent, ac veteri illi reddito nomine, Barcinonem rursus appellarent.
Durat etiam nunc hac nostra tempestate inter vrbis appendices vestigium veterum muro-
rumq; magno, sane, nec, speciosorum Quod si idem fuerint, quos construxerat Hamilcar, constat
eos in ambitu tantum quatuor valuiss, portas, currui vicinas, in quibus cælaturæ quædam
cernuntur speciem gerentes capitum boum, quibus veterum nummi significabant pacem arbi-
tramur ad laborem et exercitationem, vir omnium humanorum bonorum exorbentur in-
Frumentaria vsq; adeo vero aucta, et promixa sunt ædificia, quæ priores muros tingue,
et caput hæc vrbis esse cœperit, & nunc etiam sic Cataloniæ, vtaque sit, & pulcerio-
ribus ditioriob; amœnioribq; ac potentioribus Hispaniæ ciuitatibus. Hæc Florianus
de Campo

Athens, and, of course, in the city of Barcelona itself.

The splendid Gothic quarter, the Palau Reial, the palaces on Carrer Montcada, the Drassanes (shipyards) and several churches, such as Santa Maria del Mar, all bear witness to this glorious past.

Following its Roman birth and energetic, medieval youth, Barcelona achieved maturity in the middle of the 19th century when it embraced the industrial revolution and consolidated its position as the Spanish city of greatest European leaning. Barcelona underwent a total transformation during those years. Down came the city walls, the urban structure expanded with the creation of the Eixample, the economic profile became more industrialized and the city was culturally reborn via the Renaixença (Renaissance), which, in turn, sowed the seeds of

1 & 3. *Museu d'Història. Underground Roman ruins and Barcino stone.*
2. *Bas-relief in the Roman walls.*
4 & 5. *Romanesque church of Sant Pau del Camp. Cloister and main façade.*
6. *Gothic portal of the Town hall.*

1

2

3

4

5

6

the Modernisme movement whose magnificent fruits were harvested at the beginning of the 20th century. This was the crop that endowed the city with its most characteristic image – the most vivid impression left in the memory of its 20th century visitors.

During the last decade of this century, with the background of the 1992 Olympic Games, Barcelona has made a great leap forward. More open to the sea than ever, converted into a model of modern urban planning, culturally and economically consolidated, and decked out by both local and internationally renowned artists and architects, Barcelona has come of age as a city of reference. A reference that was first Catalan, then Mediterranean and is now, finally, Universal.

1. *The Arc de Triomf, built in 1889.*
2. *The Sagrada Família, cathedral of Modernisme.*
3. *Royal galley, Museu Marítim in the shipyards.*
4. *Aerial view of the 14th century shipyards, at the Rambla-Paral·lel cross roads, near the Columbus monument*

1

2

3

The Port
and the Rambla

The Christopher Columbus monument, with its height of fifty metres, is one of Barcelona's best-known landmarks. His index finger permanently points seaward and personifies the city's recognition of the rôle the sea has played in its history. It was, after all, the sea that brought the founders of Barcino to these shores, and across the same sea their descendants ventured out in search of wider horizons.

A walk along Barcelona's seaboard allows us to discover the

1. The port and Columbus monument.
2. The port, the Rambla del Mar and Maremàgnum.

close connections that exist between the city and the sea on a day-to-day basis. From south to north, the visitor will first come across the commercial port with its silos and warehouses from where merchandise is received and dispatched. This port is surrounded by a long breakwater, the city's ultimate protection from the sea and a favourite spot among fishermen, joggers and courting couples.

Towards the north, and facing the old city centre, lie the docks from where passenger ships sail to the Balearic Islands and other destinations. Next, a sinuous catwalk (a continuation of the Rambla) that can be raised to allow vessels to pass beneath, leads us to the Maremàgnum complex, recently built over the waters of the port as a commercial centre. During the first year of its existence, twelve million people have visited its aquarium, cinemas, shops and restaurants.

1. Monument of Christopher Columbus.
2. The lower part of the Rambla by night.

Our visit to Barcelona's coast-line continues towards the north through the re-urbanized areas which surround the Barceloneta, a populous quarter of narrow streets and markedly maritime atmosphere and, at the northernmost extreme, the Olympic village and its recreational harbour. This residential zone, built to house the athletes competing in the 1992 Olympic Games, has become one of the city's busiest spots, particularly during the spring and summer. Both the Olympic village and the Barceloneta are bordered by the well cared for beach that stretches 4 km. along the waterfront. We must return to the Columbus monument to begin our ascent of the Rambla, the customary route to the sea for Barcelona's inhabitants, and a beautiful and emblematic symbol of an open city where all cultures, races and traditions have their place.

1. The Rambla del Mar catwalk whose sinuous form connects the city and Maremàgnum.

For centuries, the Rambla was an open watercourse and the city's outlet to the sea. Today an ample avenue shaded by luxuriant plane trees, it divides the Raval from the Gothic quarter. Structured around a wide central boulevard with traffic lanes on either side, the Rambla is a river of vitality with kiosks selling newspapers, flowers and domestic animals. Wider at the lowest end, the thoroughfare reaches its mean width on a level with the Plaça Reial, a rectangular porticoed square dotted with tall palm trees and bathed by the sun. The Rambla is lined with the outdoor terraces of old cafés, establishments with Modernist façades and new souvenir shops, but perhaps the most interesting point is the Gran Teatre del Liceu, the opera house, seat of Barcelona's important tradition as a city of opera lovers whose ranks are pas-

1. The Plaça Reial, just off the Rambla.
2. Flower stalls dot the central stretch of the Rambla.
3. A classic view of the Rambla: rivers of strolling people and kiosks under the shade of the plane trees.

1

2

sionately divided between sup-
porters of Wagner and those of
Verdi. In front of the Liceu, the
pavement is decorated with a
mosaic by Joan Miró. A few
doors further up, a space has been
purposely left in a new building to
allow the Gothic church of el Pi
to be visible and form part of the
Rambla from its position in the
Ciutat Vella. On the other side
stands the impressive metallic
structure of the Boqueria market.
The coat of arms of the city is represented in leaded crystal over the
entrance which opens onto the
multicoloured world, full of vitality, of the covered market, a spectacle in itself, where fruit, vegeta-
bles, fish and crustaceans are sold.

Our walk along the Rambla
continues to its highest point at
the Plaça de Catalunya passing, on
the way, between spectacular dis-

*1. The terraces under the arcades of the
Plaça Reial.*
*2. Casa Figueras, Modernist shop on the
Rambla.*
*3, 4 & 5. Three views of the Boqueria
market with its ample range of wares,
just off the Rambla.*

1

3

4

plays of flowers outside the many stalls and characteristic "living statues", street entertainers of the most passive kind. At any hour of the day or night, the Rambla is a melting pot where all the faces of humanity are apparent. Smartly-dressed executives rub shoulders with wealthy tourists and back-packers, immigrants of many races and colours, poets, musicians, hurried messengers, illegal gamblers, vendors of contraband cigarettes, and the city's upper and middle classes on their way to the theatre or the opera.

1. *Modernist detail of the Casa Quadros (Rambla).*
2. *Fountain in the Plaça Reial.*
3. *Passers-by and human statue.*
4. *Bird stall.*
5. *Mosaic by the painter Joan Miró in the Pla de l'Os in the heart of the Rambla.*
6. *Flower stalls.*

Ciutat Vella and Gothic style

Barcelona may be compared to an old tree whose trunk has thickened over the course of two thousand years, and the core of this trunk is the Gothic quarter, situated to the right of the Rambla looking towards the Plaça de Catalunya from the sea. The streets are narrow, and the buildings, whose façades show the ravages of time and the dampness of the climate, are bathed in a golden sunlight that only reaches down to the pavements for a short time each day.

1. The cathedral and Ciutat Vella from the air.
2. Partial plan of Ciutat Vella.

1

The old part of the city, although so evidently of another era, is a thriving area and maintains its importance on many levels. It is here that both spiritual and temporal matters have their seats in the cathedral and Palau Reial, respectively. Also, the Palau de la Generalitat (headquarters of the Catalan autonomous government), The Ajuntament (Town hall), the churches of Santa Maria del Mar and del Pi, and the restored palaces on Carrer Montcada, all lie within its precincts.

A visit to the Gothic quarter may start at the Plaça Nova, a pedestrian zone in front of the cathedral where street markets are sometimes held. Building work on Barcelona's Gothic cathedral was started, as such, at the end of the thirteenth century and continued intermittently during the following six hundred years until the end of the nineteenth century when the façade was finally

1. *Remains of the Roman walls.*
2. *Main façade of the cathedral.*
3. *Detail of the cathedral cloister.*

Ciutat Vella **35** and Gothic style

2

3

completed. The temple has three groined or ribbed vaults and is flanked by two elegant octagonal towers. Magnolia, medlar, palm and orange trees grow in the adjoining cloister and these elements, along with the chapels, the murmur of the fountain and the flagstones, green with age, combine to create a magical, almost unreal atmosphere.

On leaving the cloister, the Plaça Felip Neri is another haven of peace worth visiting and, from here, we return, around the apse of the cathedral, towards the Plaça del Rei.

The Palau Reial Major, which presides the square, is steeped in history. It was within the Saló del Tinell that, allegedly, Columbus was received by the king and queen both before and after his voyage of discovery. The building itself, the heart of Catalan power

1. Cloister of the cathedral: a shaded and serene precinct.
2. In the foreground, the spires of the cathedral. In the background, those of the Temple de la Sagrada Família.

in the splendid medieval era, has been alternately converted, mutilated and restored since the final days of the Roman Empire. The façade of the palace (formed by different sequences of arches that add the finishing touches to the Rei Martí tower), and the Renaissance staircase, are particularly impressive. The palace is flanked, to the left by the Palau del Lloctinent and, to the right, by the chapel of Santa Àgueda. On the far side of the square, next to a modern sculpture by Eduardo Chillida whose form harmonises perfectly with the medieval architecture, lies the Museu d'Història de la Ciutat. From the museum, an underground passageway leads through the ruins of the Roman city beneath the aforementioned buildings and the Museu Marès.

The nearby street, named Carrer d'Argenteria – once the home

---

1 & 2. Two views of the cathedral: top of a pinnacle and interior of a spire.
3 & 4. Detail and general view of "L'Ou com balla", an Easter tradition repeated each year in the cathedral cloister.

1

2

3

of silversmiths and makers of steel weapons as its name suggests, – used to be called Carrer del Mar. At the far end, and almost on the seafront, lies the Plaça de Santa Maria del Mar with its markedly medieval atmosphere dominated by the church of the same name. Built by Berenguer de Montagut during the first half of the fourteenth century, Santa Maria is a paradigm of Catalan Gothic architecture. The interior, distributed in three very tall naves, exudes a sensation of majesty and elegance, due both to the svelteness of the columns and the great distance between them.

Behind Santa Maria del Mar, close to the old market on the Passeig del Born, lies Carrer Montcada where Barcelona's nobility built their palaces in the fourteenth and fifteenth centuries. This street is a succession of opulent mansions, illuminated obliquely by the sun's rays and

1. The Torre del Rei Martí, in the Plaça del Rei.
2. Interior of the Gothic Saló del Tinell.

1

with ample porches to allow the passage of horse-drawn carriages. Behind these grand entrances there is usually a spacious patio and staircase leading to the first floor of the residence. These palaces have been converted into art galleries and museums in recent times and, among them, of particular importance is the Museu Picasso which today occupies three adjoining palaces. Its permanent collection of the artist's work (with special emphasis on his earlier years), has made this one of the most visited tourist attractions in the city. Just opposite lies the Museu de la Indumentària (Costume Museum), and the recently inaugurated seat of the Barbier Mueller collection of ancient art.

Via the neighbouring Carrer Princesa and Carrer Ferràn, one arrives at the Plaça de Sant Jaume. In this square, reminiscent of an Italian *piazza*, the two important

*1. Church and Plaça Sant Felip Neri.
2 & 3. Two views of the Carrer del Bisbe: access to the Plaça Sant Jaume and opening into the Plaça Nova.*

1

2

3

political powers that govern Barcelona are to be found. They face one another symbolically from the two extremes. On one side the Generalitat (or Catalan autonomous government) and, on the other, the Ajuntament (or City Hall).

The Palau de la Generalitat building dates, in its earliest construction, from the beginning of the fifteenth century. The most outstanding elements, the patio and principal staircase, the façade overlooking Carrer del Bisbe Irurita, or the Pati dels Tarongers, follow the Gothic style. The main façade over the Plaça de Sant Jaume is Renaissance.

The Town hall is also fruit of numerous transformations. Its most characteristic element is, probably, the Saló de Cent where the representatives of the city would meet towards the end of the

1. Patio of the Museu de la Indumentària in an old palace on Carrer Montcada.
2 & 3. The Plaça del Pi becomes, successively, an art market and a musical scenario.

1

2

3

fourteenth century and which the municipal authorities still use today for meetings of special relevance. The Plaça de Sant Jaume, flanked by the seats of these two institutions, is the scene of many kinds of demonstrations and gatherings: from fervent manifestations of patriotism to the celebration of sporting victories by local teams, organised dancing of *sardanes* – the typical Catalan folk dance – and the building of *castells*, or human towers.

1 & 2. "Castellers" in action: the rise and fall of a human tower in the Plaça Sant Jaume.
3. View of the Palau de la Generalitat, seat of the Catalan autonomous government.

The Eixample and Modernisme

The Eixample, basically a residential area, forms the heart of modern Barcelona. Until the middle of the 19th century, the city was constricted by the structure of the medieval walls. In 1856, the engineer Ildefons Cerdà presented his first project for the widening of the city, a visionary plan which would enable the configuration of the city to adapt to both present and future needs. In synthesis, the Eixample could be defined as the rational adaptation of the space between the old city centre and the outlying villages with optimum

1. Aerial view of the Eixample.
2. Partial plan of the Eixample.

conditions for traffic, salubrity, and, above all, population density. This plan completely revolutionized the standards of the day and now, on the threshold of the 21st century, is still viable.

The Eixample is a striking example of Catalan *seny*, an idiom meaning good sense or judgement, often applied to the Catalan people and their philosophy of life. The Modernisme movement appropriately undertook the decoration of this new creation by means of the use of stone, ceramics, wrought iron and stained glass, thus combining *seny* with *rauxa*, the exuberant and ebullient contrasting facet of the Catalan character.

On paper, the Eixample forms a gridded web of right-angled quadrangles, interrupted only by the principal thoroughfares: the stately Passeig de Gràcia (where, at

1, 2 & 3. Fountains and sculptures in the Plaça de Catalunya.
4. Aerial view of the Plaça de Catalunya.
5. La Pedrera, by Gaudí, on the Passeig de Gràcia.
6. The marathon, on the Passeig de Gràcia.
7. The Sagrada Família and the Diagonal.

the beginning of this century, the city's inhabitants used to stroll and gossip), Carrer Aragó and the Gran Via de les Corts Catalanes (which cross it longitudinally), the Avinguda Diagonal (which crosses it obliquely), the Rambla (the liveliest of them all), and a few squares, such as the Plaça de Catalunya.

When the majority of the Eixample's buildings were constructed, Catalunya was experiencing a time of affluence that started at the beginning of the 19th century when Barcelona was emerging as the country's economic motor, and was consolidated by the industrial revolution and the feverish activity of Catalan factories during the first decades of the 20th, when they became the foremost suppliers to those European nations involved in the First World War. This economic bonanza, together with cultural tendencies such as the Renaixença and the resurgence of

1. The quadrangles of the Eixample, crossed by the Diagonal.
2. The Casa de les Punxes.

1

the applied arts, coincided with, and reinforced, the Modernisme movement in all its aspects.

Barcelona is not only the city of Gaudí, an inspired and unclassifiable figure, but also of Modernisme itself, the architectural style which may be described as the harmonious coexistence between dozens of architects, hundreds of promoters and thousands of craftsmen, all working together.

In the city of Barcelona, Modernisme (in accordance with the above description), displays its most emblematic works, and the key figures behind its creation are on constant exhibition, to a degree unsurpassed elsewhere. The foremost example is, undoubtedly, the Palau de la Música Catalana (Sant Pere més alt, 11), the work of Lluís Domènech i Montaner. Built between 1905 and 1908 as seat of the Orfeó Català choral society, the Palau is one of the most beautiful

1 & 2. Palau de la Música Catalana, by Domènech i Montaner. Access colonnade and interior view of the concert hall with Modernist decoration.

1

and overwhelming concert halls in the world. Conceived with total freedom of expression, despite the limited dimensions of the site, it is a display of architecture in which technical audacity, symbolism and rich craftsmanship all play their part. Floral and polychromatic, magical and welcoming, the Palau is full of vitality and offers some three hundred concerts each year which are attended by half a million people.

The sum of professional effort and the desire to create a work of art in its totality, characterizes the Palau and are constant factors in all the Modernist architecture to be found in Barcelona. It is apparent in other works by Domènech i Montaner; among them, the Hospital de Sant Pau (Sant Antoni Maria Claret, 167-171) and the Casa Lleó Morera (Passeig de Gràcia, 35). But, as has already been

1. *Main façade, Palau de la Música.*
2. *Mosaic.*
3. *Box office.*
4. *Main façade.*
5. *Sculptures and mosaics on the stage.*

1

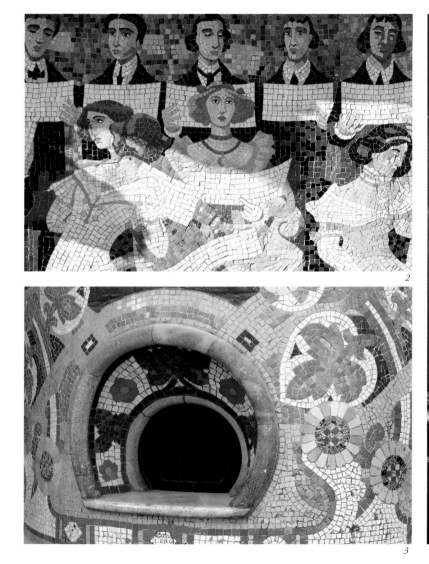

2

3

4

mentioned, Modernisme is not just the work of a few architects, but a movement in which, to differing degrees, many and diverse social sectors are represented.

Other Modernist works of particular interest should, therefore, be mentioned: the Casa Amatller (Passeig de Gràcia, 41) and the Casa de les Punxes (Diagonal, 416-420), both by Josep Puig i Cadafalch; and also some of the works by Jujol, Rubió i Bellver, Valeri i Pupurull, Granell, Sayrach, Sagnier, etc. At the same time, it should not be forgotten that a stroll through the Eixample, together with a more detailed study of the more important examples, allows the visitor to enjoy, in a more relaxed and informal manner, the continuous discovery of the splendid building traditions of that time, whether in the form of a great monumental construction or a humble shop

1. Aerial view of the Hospital de Sant Pau.
2, 3 & 4. Three reflections of Modernisme: Casa Amatller, Palau Macaia and Casa Comalat.

2

3

4

front. Hidden architectural treasures may be found in balconies, shop windows, mosaics, cornices, halls, staircases or lifts, if the visitor takes the time to seek them out. Treasures that may be admired from the street itself, but do not end there: some interiors may be visited occasionally (the Casa Lleó Morera, for example). Within, the visitor will come across a wealth of authentic craftsmanship, true masterpieces of the applied arts.

This creative abundance, visible both at street level and within the interiors of the buildings, placed Barcelona at the forefront of the great Modernist cities of Europe, such as Paris, London, Munich or Vienna, all of which enjoyed a period of particular splendour at the end of the nineteenth century and the beginning of the twentieth.

1 & 3. Casa Lleó Morera. Detail of a mosaic and view of the stained-glass windows.
2. Lift by J.M. Jujol.

1

2

The world of Gaudí

The image of Barcelona is closely associated with that of the architect Antoni Gaudí. The discovery of his work is one of the principle objectives of many visitors to the city. La Pedrera (Passeig de Gràcia, 92) is, perhaps, the most suitable starting point for the circuit of Gaudí's Barcelona. This residential building (currently property of a cultural foundation and used for exhibitions), lies on a corner of the Eixample and has three façades which, in reality, form one single frontage,

1 & 2. La Pedrera. Detail of the façade, cut stone and wrought iron.
3. Roof of La Pedrera at dusk.

defined by characteristic curved lines which evoke an improbable wave of stone, peppered by the twisted metal rails of the balconies.

Following an extremely costly refurbishment, finished in the mid nineties, La Pedrera offers a magnificent aspect, and not only from the outside, as the frescoes that decorate the accesses to the stairwell have been returned to their original, brilliant colours. Many of the apartments have regained their initial appearance and again proudly display the Modernist woodwork and curious painting and reliefs traced on the plaster ceilings. On the highest level, the building reserves one of its greatest surprises, the stunning spectacle of the roof. The forest of chimney stacks, the imaginative sculptures that camouflage the accesses to the stairways and water tanks, the ondulating surface and the inventive ornamentation, comprise a unique architectural ensemble, conceivable only to an ingenious mind. The old

1, 2, 3 & 4. Details of La Pedrera.
5 & 6. Casa Batlló. Staircase and detail of façade.

1

2

3

4

5

6

attics (another singular area whose structure resembles that of the belly of a gigantic sea monster), have been fitted out for exhibitions of scale models, photographs and videos with the aim of giving an insight into the internal logic of Gaudí's work, his methods, ambitions, historical context and points of reference. His genius did not only reside in his incredible finishing touches, but also, and primarily, in his innovative and even visionary proposals in the fields of building and construction. Not far from La Pedrera stands another famous Gaudí edifice, the Casa Batlló (Passeig de Gràcia, 43). His work on this house – starting from a building of little interest – consisted in the addition of two new floors, the reconstruction of the first floor and the complete transformation of the exterior. Curvaceous lines dominate the façade, adorned with organic elements and coated with many

1, 2 & 3. Rooftop and chimneys of the Casa Batlló.
4. Nocturnal view of the balcony and lower floors of the Casa Batlló.

colours reminiscent of brocades and precious stones. The roof (which resembles the skin of a dragon), crowned by a bulbous cross and several chimneys, accentuates the medieval atmosphere of the ensemble.

Both the Pedrera and the Casa Batlló are the works of an unbounded imagination. They have, however, owing to their situation between other buildings, limitations in size not applicable to other works by Gaudí, the most eloquent example of ambitious dimensions being the Temple de la Sagrada Família (Marina, 252 / Plaça Sagrada Família).

Gaudí, a man of mystical leaning and spiritual convictions, worked on the Sagrada Família – where work continues today amid religious fervour and the protests of architects – with greater determination and no less freedom than he had shown in his other undertakings. In fact, he spent the last years of his life close

1 & 2. Sagrada Família. View of the four pinnacles of the Nativity façade and the Passion façade with its new sculptural groups.

to the temple where one of the outbuildings was converted for use as his living quarters.

The Sagrada Família – as Barcelona's second cathedral – is a structure of uncommon dimensions. Conceived in the form of a Latin cross with five naves, three façades, an apse and a transept, the temple is famous for its slender towers, which soar nearly one hundred metres over the building and are crowned by ceramic pinnacles. These spires combine both modern, almost aeronautical, lines and overelaborate ornamentation to produce a highly spectacular result which, curiously, is not the most exaggerated of Gaudí's intentions for this work. A monumental cupola, nearly one hundred and seventy metres high, figures among the parts of the church still to be completed and this dome will become the most outstanding feature of this colossal architectural creation.

1. Sagrada Família. Coronation of Mary.
2 & 4. Staircases in the spires.
3. Relief of the Annunciation, in the crypt.

Gaudí was thirty-one years old when he accepted the commission to build the Sagrada Família and spent the rest of his life bound to this work which progressed discontinuously, much as it does today, totally dependant on the availability of funds. Here he gave free rein to his creativity and allowed his imagination to fly much further than is usually mandatory in buildings of a religious nature.

Imagination is also a dominant factor in the Park Güell, Gaudí's largest creation in Barcelona, and the principal work assigned to him by his patron. This garden city, with an area of approximately three hectares, combines the labours of urban planning, architecture and art. It lies beyond the limits of the Eixample and the buildings described previously, but the abundance of surprises to be found within the park's precinct more

1. Park Güell. Aerial view.
2. Serpentine bench.
3. The entrance pavilions.
4 & 5. Hypostyle chamber which supports the main square.

1

3

4

than warrant a visit. The entrance (on Carrer Olot), is flanked by two houses, integrated in the stone wall and reserved for the guardians or porters of the estate and visitors. From this entrance there is a splendid view of the monumental staircase which gives access to the park proper, adorned by an out-standing ceramic dragon. Behind the staircase lies the hypostyle chamber – a forest of pillars – and, overhead, the great Plaça del Park Güell, from where magnificent views of Barcelona may be observed. Around the perimeter of the square, the famous serpentine bench, adorned with pieces of bro-ken tiles, plates and bottles which make up a seemingly endless, dynamic collage of dazzling colour. Having discovered these central focus points, the visitor will come across many more during the course of a walk through the rest of the park, particularly in the

1. Porticoed gallery with slanting columns.
2, 3 & 4. Details of ceramic facing.
5. Staircase to the hypostyle chamber, presided over by the dragon.

1

2

3

4

porched galleries and the residences of both the Güell family and Gaudí himself, all of which accentuate the prevailing dreamlike, magical ambience.

Those visitors who wish to complete the Gaudí circuit in Barcelona should also visit the Casa Vicens (Carolines, 18-24), the Finca Güell pavilions (Avda. de Pedralbes, 7), the Palau Güell (Nou de Rambla, 9), the convent of the Teresians (Ganduxer, 85-105), the Casa Calvet (Casp, 48), the Bellesguard tower (Bellesguard, 16-20), the gateway and railings of the Miralles estate (Manuel Girona, 55-61), and the schools of the Sagrada Família (next door to the temple). Although a short journey out of Barcelona is required, it would be a pity not to see the sensational and tremendously expressive crypt of the Colònia Güell in Santa Coloma de Cervelló, completed by Gaudí in 1915.

Works by Gaudí:
1. Convent of the Teresians.
2 & 3. Torre Bellesguard.
4. Balcony of the Casa Calvet.
5 & 6. Casa Vicens.

1

2

3

4

5

6

The Olympic city

Just after nightfall on the evening of 25th July 1992, a flaming arrow left its wake in the sky over Barcelona. Hundreds of millions of viewers all over the world held their breath for an instant until it arrived at its target and lit the flame over the Montjuïc Olympic Stadium. This moment marked, not only the inauguration of the XXV Olympic Games, but also a new Barcelona, lovingly reconstructed for the occasion.

1. The Poble Espanyol and, in the background, the Palau Nacional and the Olympic ring.
2. View of the stadium during the 1992 Olympic Games.

Barcelona's Olympic modernisation consists, schematically, of the general renovation of the city, the recuperation of its seaboard, the radical transformation of four areas (classified as "Olympic") located at the four corners of the city, and the creation of the new Rondes, or ring roads, which circumvent the city, reorganise the traffic and redefine hitherto established patterns.

The Olympic area, par excellence, is situated at Montjuïc, scenario of the major sporting competitions of the 1992 Games. The mountain of Montjuïc, which overlooks the port, is the city's traditional, natural defence, as is apparent from the fort that stands at the top. In 1929, at the time of the International Exhibition, the mountain underwent a degree of development which

1. Nighttime illumination of the Montjuïc fountains and the Palau Nacional.
2. Inauguration ceremony in the Olympic stadium.
3. View of the Olympic ring, with the stadium in the foreground.

1

2

left in its wake a great deal of classical architecture (with exceptions such as the visionary German pavilion built by Mies van Rohe), winding avenues and romantic gardens. In 1992, this development was completed with the building of the Olympic ring.

This area, designed by the architects Correa and Milà, assembles the principal Olympic installations around an esplanade of classic shape and symmetry. The most important element is the Olympic stadium itself, built by the same architects, together with the Italian Gregotti, based on an already existent construction whose exterior was left intact, whereas the interior was totally refurbished. Next to the stadium stands the Palau Sant Jordi, an indoor sports arena designed by the Japanese Arata Isozaki, whose roof vaguely

1. Sculptural group "Utsurohi" (Aiko Miyawaki), in front of the Palau Sant Jordi (Arata Isozaki), to the left, in the Olympic ring. In the background, the white silhouette of the communications tower designed by Santiago Calatrava,

1

recalls the shell of a tortoise. The Olympic swimming pools and a sports university flank the remaining sides of the great esplanade. The white communications tower, work of Santiago Calatrava, completes the ensemble of the Olympic ring, whose characteristics are those of an airy, open space where the sky seems to be a little closer to the Earth; a space reminiscent of the horizontal cities of antiquity, as opposed to the vertical tendencies of present day building. Just as the Olympic ring put the final touches to the development of Montjuïc, the Olympic village transformed Barcelona's seafront. In spite of being the greatest of all the Mediterranean capitals, Barcelona has always maintained a somewhat distant relationship with the sea. The port, to the south, and the manufacturing quarter of Poble Nou, to the north, effectively separated it from the rest of the city's inhabitants. The 1992 Games also revolutionised this relationship as they gave rise to the substitution

of the old, obsolete Poble Nou factories for the modern residential area of the Olympic village, accommodation for the world's greatest athletes for three weeks and now one of the city's most dynamic neighbourhoods.

Four kilometres of beaches, two skyscrapers, a recreational port, a new district whose brick buildings evoke the old industrial traditions of the zone, and a park, are some of the characteristic elements of Barcelona's second Olympic area where, perhaps, the greatest change of all has taken place. During the summer, the beaches, accessible almost by the Underground, are packed with hundreds of thousands of citizens. The restaurants and bars of the Olympic port are among the busiest in the city all year round, and their terraces are crowded from spring until the end of autumn.

1, 2 & 3. Views of the Olympic village, 4. Detail of the sculpture "Fish" by Frank O. Gehry, in front of one of the Olympic village skyscrapers.

1

2

3

The quartet of Olympic areas created for the 1992 Games is completed by the Valle Hebrón and Diagonal centres. Their new sports facilities are well worth visiting for the revolutionary concepts apparent in both their decorative elements and the sculpture park.

The Rondes should be mentioned as the final fruit of the Olympic transformation, as their thirty-five kilometres of ring roads have modified and lightened the heavy burden of traffic within the city. However, the effect of the Olympic Games should not just be measured by these direct results and is perceptible all over the city, particularly in the Eixample and other historic zones, thanks to the cleanup operation that was initiated before the Games and has continued ever since.

1. Aerial view of the Olympic village and port, Barcelona's new seafront, with the Hotel Arts and Torre Mapfre

The city of the arts

Pablo Picasso spent many of his formative years in Barcelona, the city that also gave birth to Joan Miró and Antoni Tàpies. These great artistic figures of the twentieth century have prolonged the ancestral link between Barcelona and the plastic arts. The beauty of the city lies in both the refined talent of artists and craftsmen, present in many different buildings, and the wealth of the artistic heritage which may be admired in the abundant museums and collections. The city's foremost museum is the Museu Nacional d'Art de Catalunya

1. The Palau Nacional, seat of the MNAC.
2. The great oval hall, Palau Nacional.

1

(MNAC), located in the Palau Nacional de Montjuïc. This centre, refurbished by Gae Aulenti, houses the most important collection of Romanesque mural painting in the world. At the beginning of this century, many works were retrieved from churches in the Pyrenean mountain villages and brought here for safekeeping in a conscientious campaign to save them from deterioration. At the same time, the museum possesses a valuable collection of Gothic painting, and more recent works which are exhibited in the Museu d'Art Modern de la Ciutadella. Aside from the artistic treasures housed within its walls, the MNAC is an interesting building in itself, and the dimensions of its oval hall are quite unmatched.

Apart from the heritage of ancient and classical art, which

1. "Paisatge de Fornalutx" by J. Sunyer.
2. The Mare de Déu dels Angels, altar piece from Tortosa, by Pere Serra.
3. Three-piece cabinet with decorative panels, by Gaspar Homar.
4. Pantocrator from the Romanesque mural of the church of Santa Maria de Taüll. (All these works belong to the MNAC).

1

2

3

includes the Thyssen Bornemisza collection on show in the magnificent Monestir de Pedralbes, Barcelona is also rich in modern and contemporary works. In the heart of the old Raval stands the impressive Museu d'Art Contemporani de Barcelona (MACBA), recently built by the American architect Richard Meier. The luminous white bulk of the building houses the most recent creations of both Catalan and foreign contemporary artists.

The Raval district is undergoing a process of transformation and, recently, several new art galleries specialising in the work of young artists have opened here. Close to the MACBA lies the Centre de Cultura Contemporània de Barcelona whose programme of exhibitions is always related to the modern city and is one of the most attractive and imaginative in Barcelona.

1. *Monastery of Pedralbes.*
2. *"El desconsol", by J. Llimona.*
3. *"Elogio del agua", by E. Chillida.*
4. *Centre de Cultura Contemporània de Barcelona.*

1

2

3

Despite all this fierce competition, the most-visited museum in the city is the one dedicated exclusively to the work of Pablo Picasso, situated in three adjacent palaces on Carrer Montcada. As mentioned in the previous chapter, it houses the best collection of his formative years, along with important works of later eras. The paintings, which offer many examples of the successive revolutions imposed by Picasso on pictorial art, contrast sharply with the medieval surroundings of the museum. Apart from the permanent collection, the Museu Picasso regularly offers temporary exhibitions dedicated to different periods or themes of the artist's work.

In the heart of the Eixample, the Fundació Tàpies (Aragó, 255), houses a splendid collection donated to the city by this Barcelona-born artist and many other exhibitions, and is renowned for its marked personali-

1. The German pavilion from the International Exposition of 1929, and built by Mies van der Rohe is a key piece in contemporary architecture.
2. Exterior aspect of the MACBA, by the American architect Richard Meier.

1

ty and notable commitment to the arts. The building is an old Modernist construction whose brick façade is crowned by a huge, controversial sculpture by Tàpies that cannot pass unnoticed by pedestrians on the busy street corner below.

Up on the Montjuïc hill stands yet another centre dedicated to a great Catalan artist: the Fundació Miró, a private institution instigated by the express wish of the painter, not only with the aim of showing his own work, but also that of young artists. The Fundació is situated in a luminous building of clearly Mediterranean influence where the hustle and bustle of the city seems to be held at bay by its solid concrete walls. Here, paintings, sculptures and tapestries representative of Miró's complete works are on permanent show, along with other, temporary exhibitions.

Apart from those mentioned here, many more galleries and foun-

1. Nocturnal view of the fundació Tàpies, crowned by the work "Núvol i cadira".
2 & 3. Two works on show in the Museu Picasso: "Busto de mujer con sombrero" and "Arlequín".

1

2

3

dations (either publicly or privately funded), exist in the city, and art lovers will find an endless list of shows and exhibitions at any time of the year.

But art can be found in Barcelona without ever setting foot in a museum or gallery, on the streets themselves. The Columbus monument, at the end of the Rambla, is one of the city's marks of identity and perhaps the best known of the more than five hundred sculptures and architectural ornaments to be found in the open air. A list of these works, built in their majority during the nineteenth century (with many more additions during the last few years), includes very interesting pieces by both local and foreign artists. Outstanding among them are: the spectacular Modernist lampposts on Passeig de Gràcia (Pere Falqués), *El Desconsol* (Llimona), in the Parc de la Ciutadella opposite the seat of the Catalan parliament, *Elogio del agua* (Chillida), in the Parc de la Creueta del Coll, the aforementioned *Núvol i cadira* (Tàpies),

1 & 2. Sculptures by Miró, outside and inside the Fundació.
3. The Fundació Miró.

1

2

on top of the Fundació Tàpies on Carrer Aragó, *Dona i ocell* (Miró), in the Parc del Escorxador, the *Fish* (Gehry), in the Olympic village, and *Matches* (Oldenburg) in Vall d'Hebron.

The programme of open air sculpture carried out in Barcelona in recent years has been described by the critic Robert Hughes as "the most ambitious in the western world" and a "unique anthology". Combined with the simultaneous architectural boom, the city has undergone a new cosmopolitan expansion. Barcelona's traditional reputation as a city of the arts has now been confirmed, and even heightened, by these renewed undertakings.

1. The Bac de Roda bridge, by Santiago Calatrava.
2. The Teatre Nacional de Catalunya, by Ricardo Bofill.
3. The Collserola communications tower, by Sir Norman Foster.
4. "Dona i ocell", by Joan Miró.
5. Estació del Nord park, by Beverly Pepper.
6. "Barcelona Head", by Roy Lichtenstein.
7. Towers in the Espanya Industrial park, by Luis Peña Ganchegui.
8. "Matches", by Claes Oldenburg.

1

2

3

4

5

6

7

8

The city of leisure

The Catalans in general are known to be hard-working people, and the inhabitants of Barcelona are no exception to this rule. But they also like to enjoy themselves and, to this end, have created a great number of places in which to do so. In fact, the city is presided by two amusement parks: one on the side of the Montjuïc hill, and the Parc del Tibidabo, in the Collserola hills, from where the view of the city stretches out at one's feet as far as the sea. The Tibidabo, with its watchtower, miniature aeroplane,

1. Tibidabo fairground.
2. The Camp Nou, F. C. Barcelona's stadium.

ghost train, robot museum and other fairground attractions, is an intrinsic part of the childhood of every barcelonès.

As they grow up, they turn their interests to other fields, many of them choosing to channel their enthusiasm towards the *Fútbol Club Barcelona* – *"el Barça"* in colloquial terms – . More than just a football team, this is an enormous institution that traditionally represents both sport and the political assertion of Catalunya's identity as a nation within the Spanish state. Nearly 120,000 people attend every match played in the Camp Nou, the club's magnificent ground, and spend the rest of the week debating the result! The club's museum, where all the team's trophies are proudly exhibited, receives more than half a million visitors each year.

Barcelona abounds in bars, discotheques and nightclubs, many of which have appeared

1. "Nocturnal design": Torres de Ávila.
2 & 3. Inmates of the zoo: three dolphins and "Floquet de Neu", the albino gorilla.

1

2

3

during the last twenty years, increasing the city's already ample repertoire. Many of the most recent additions are prime examples of the high standard of the contemporary Catalan designers who have obviously inherited much of the creativity and imagination made manifest by their forefathers in the great transformation of the city at the end of the nineteenth century. The renowned Catalan cuisine, whose wide spectrum embraces both the humble *pa amb tomàquet* (bread with tomato and olive oil), and the most sophisticated creations, may be sampled at many of the hundreds of restaurants scattered over the city. International cuisine of a high standard is also widely available, along with more informal *tapas* bars.

There are two places of interest to animal lovers in Barcelona: the zoo, situated in the Parc de la Ciutadella (also site of the splendid Modernist Museu de Zoologia), is

1. *Octopus.*
2. *Observation tunnel in l'Aquàrium.*

home to the world-famous *Floquet de Neu* (Snowflake), the only example of albino gorilla in captivity. The second is l'Aquàrium, one of the attractions of the Maremàgnum commercial centre in the port. Species of fish from all over the world are housed here, and of special interest, a group of sharks may be observed at leisure, and in safety, through the walls of a transparent tunnel that crosses the floor of the great tank where they live. Another field of the arts highly represented in Barcelona is music. Apart from the opera season in the Gran Teatre del Liceu (in itself an institution, steeped in the history of the city), there are three classical music seasons and countless concerts and recitals. There are around one hundred cinemas, including Imax in the Maremàgnum centre, and some twenty theatres where both classical and avant-garde productions are per-

1. *Giant prawn, by Mariscal, on the Moll de la Fusta.*
2. *L'Illa-Diagonal commercial centre.*
3. *The IMAX cinema, Maremàgnum .*
4. *The Poble Espanyol, Montjuïc.*

formed, the latter being particularly frequent. And, of course, as befits a modern city, Barcelona has much to offer in the way of shopping, an increasingly popular pastime in this day and age. There are several principal areas including the elegant Passeig de Gràcia (El Corte Inglés department store, Virgin, the Boulevard Rosa arcade, Vinçon etc.), Avda. Diagonal (L'Illa commercial centre with FNAC, Marks & Spencer, Decathlon etc.).

In recent times, many new parks and open spaces have been either created or reclaimed for public use. They provide oases of peace and quiet where visitors and locals alike can find welcome respite from the crowded city. On the Montjuïc hill, the Poble Espanyol, built for the 1929 International Exhibition, is a curious scale model of a village, where the typical architecture of all the Spanish provinces is represented.

Barcelona is also a wonderful scenario for witnessing the many

1 to 3. Images of the "Bestiari", present in the city streets during many festivities.
4. A dragon in the Rambla.

1

2

3

manifestations of the popular folklore and traditions of Catalunya. The Catalan character – collective effort, solidarity, tenacity and a touch of madness – is probably best reflected by the *castells,* or lofty towers built by several tiers of people standing on one another's shoulders while a multitude gathers around the base, lending both physical and moral support. In a more frivolous vein are the *gegants*, or giants, and the *correfoc*, a procession of pagan origin with fire and gunpowder, both of which can be seen in towns and villages all over the country.

The *correfoc*, closely linked to the celebration of the summer solstice, turns the streets of Barcelona into a sea of fire, where lights, flames, sparks and flashes fill the night with brilliant colour. It is, at the same time, an analogy of the briefness of life and human experience and their influence on local character: pragmatic, negotiating and relativist.

1. Scenes of the "correfoc".
2 to 4. "Gegants" and other figures of the celebrations.
5. The demons of the "correfoc".

2

3

4

Environs of Barcelona

A tremendous spectrum of tourist attractions exists within a radius of two hundred kilometres of the city of Barcelona.

To the north, travellers can choose between the Pyrenees and the Costa Brava, both of which offer endless possibilities all year round. The Pyrenees present the chance to admire some of Europe's finest Romanesque churches, within easy reach of the many ski resorts where both Alpine and Nordic skiing are possible in sur-

1. Romanesque hermitage of Sant Climent de Taüll.
2. The Pedraforca mountain.
3. Rafting on the Noguera Pallaresa river.
4. Mountain trail on Mont-Rebei, Lleida.

1

2

3

4

roundings of breathtaking natural beauty, not forgetting the rivers where many adventure sports such as white-water rafting are practised. The Costa Brava, with its rugged landscape and benign climate, is much appreciated as a holiday centre. It is ideal for both water-sports enthusiasts and those who prefer to dedicate their leisure time to sunbathing and relaxation. There are many enchanting towns along the coastline, such as Cadaqués and Calella de Palafrugell, where old-style traditions rub shoulders with modern facilities.

At the same time, the Costa Brava has a rich cultural heritage, the Museu Dalí in Figueres being one of the most visited centres. Here, a great collection of the surrealist artist's work is housed, and a visit to this museum forms part of a Dalí circuit, along with his houses at Port Lligat and Púbol.

1. *Cala del Pi, near Platja d'Aro.*
2. *Calella de Palafrugell.*
3. *Lateen-sail regatta with Cadaqués in the background.*
4. *The Torre Galatea, Museu Dalí in Figueres.*

Closer to Barcelona lies the impressive massif of Montserrat, carved and eroded by wind and rain over the centuries, and considered by the Catalan people to be a holy mountain and spiritual centre where the image of the Black Madonna, patron saint of Catalunya, is venerated.

The Monestir de Montserrat with its splendid basilica, is home to a notable library and an art collection which includes contemporary works. The unmistakable silhouette of Montserrat, rising abruptly from the plain and visible for miles, is one of Catalunya's most emblematic symbols. South of Barcelona lies the attractive wine-growing region of Penedès, world-famous for its *cava* (local equivalent of champagne). On its coast, the towns of Sitges and Cambrils have been internationally popular resorts for many years.

1

2

3

1, 2 & 3. Three views of Montserrat: the monastery, the Sant Jeroni funicular, and the profile of the mountain from the plain.

Also to the south of the city, three important monasteries are to be found: Poblet, Santes Creus and Vallbona de les Monges, all of great importance to both the secular and spiritual history of the country.

Of a very different nature, the Port Aventura theme park, situated between Salou and Vilaseca, has taken its place among Catalunya's many attractions. The millions of people who have flocked here since its inauguration in 1995 have made it the second most visited centre of its kind in Europe.

In short, Catalunya offers the visitor a wide and often simultaneous spectrum of possibilities: from natural beauty spots to service industries, from winter sports to the pleasures of summer by the sea, from consumer goods to culture, all fruit of privileged resources and several decades of dedication to the development of the tourist industry.

1. Port Aventura: the "Dragon Khan".
2. The Cistercian monastery at Poblet.
3. The port of Cambrils.